Dedication

For our children:

Kathryn, Nigel and Emily Hollins and Abigail Witchalls

Ben, Rachel, Yoni, Abi and Aviva Sireling

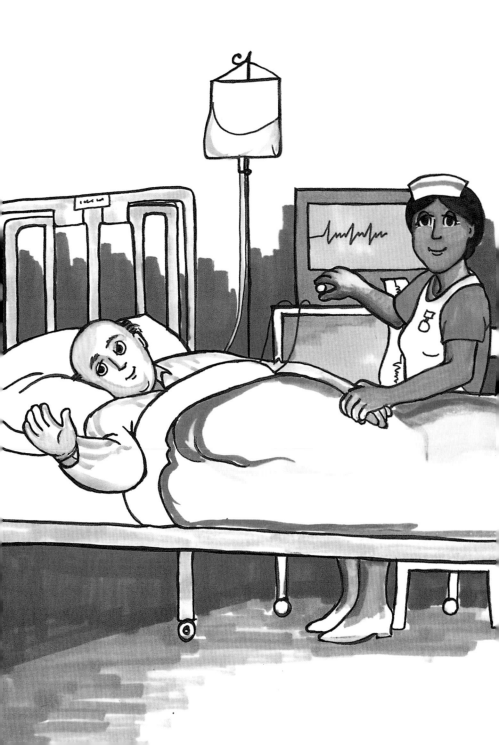

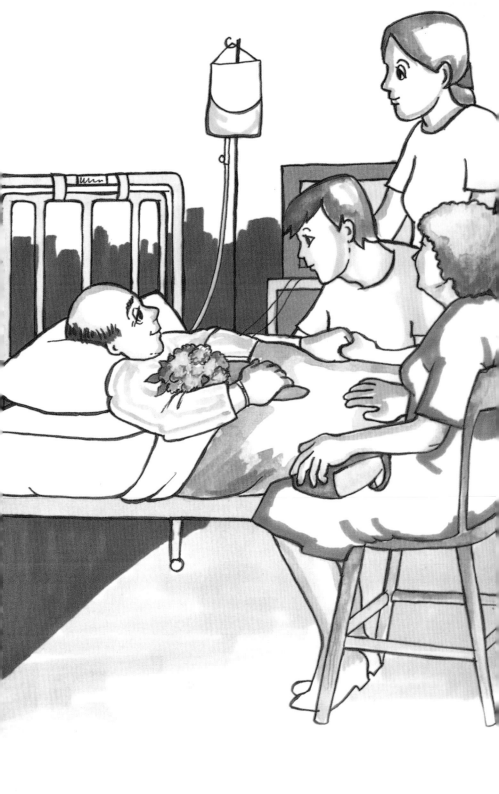

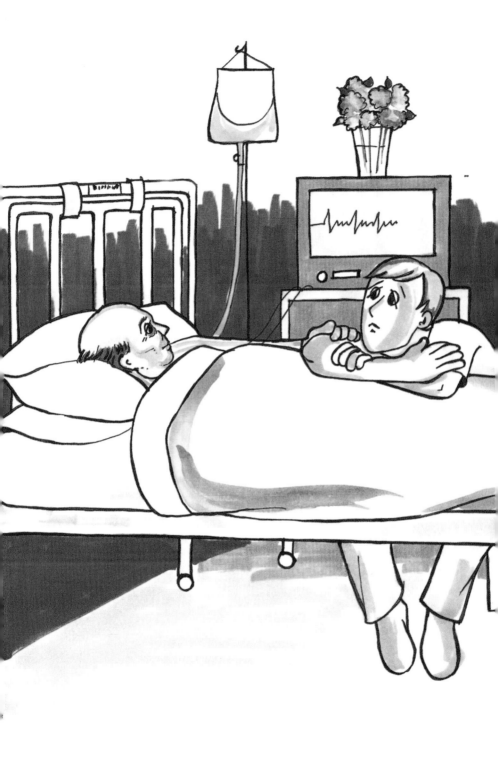

13

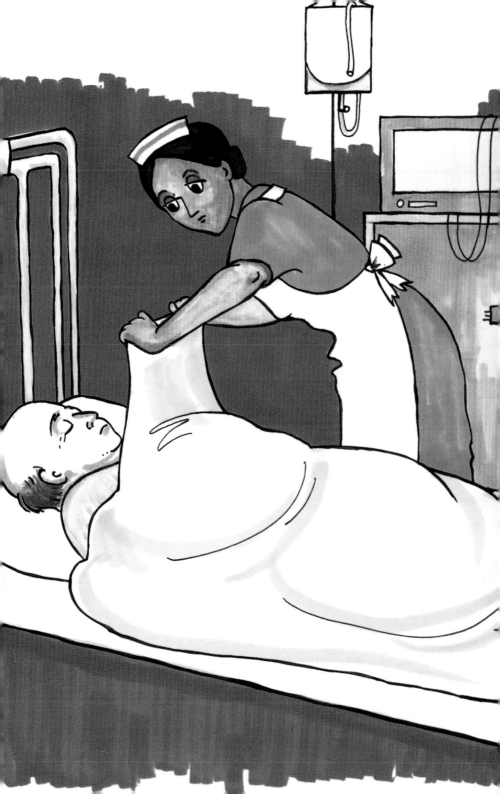

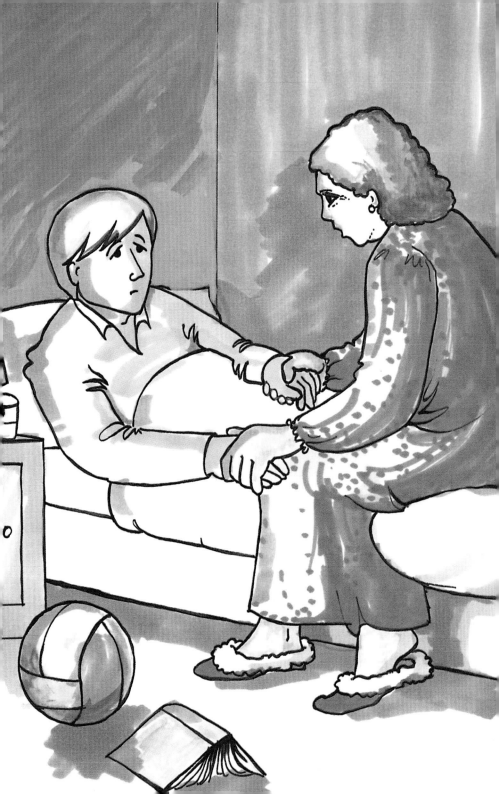

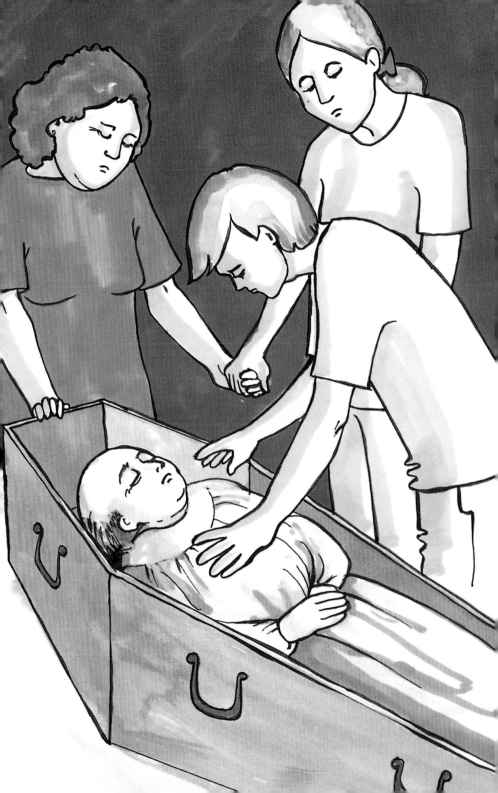

23

The following words are provided for people who want a ready-made story rather than tell their own

1. This is a picture of Stephen with his family. The story tells us what happened when his Dad died.

2. One day Dad had a pain.

3. Mum phoned 999 for an ambulance.

4. The ambulance came quickly and took Dad to hospital.

5. Stephen and Julie went to hospital to see Dad.

6. They bought some flowers to cheer him up.

7. Dad was in bed because he was ill. A nurse was looking after him.

8. Dad was happy to see them. They didn't know what to say. Soon Dad got tired. That was because he was ill.

9. That evening Mum said "Let's turn off the television and talk about Dad." Stephen didn't feel like talking. He just wanted Dad to get better.

10. Dad was very ill. He slept most of the time. Stephen sat next to his bed. He wanted to be with his Dad. Sometimes his Dad woke up and looked at him.

11. Stephen kissed his Dad. He wanted to say goodbye.

12. Mum said "I'm worried about Dad. I don't think he'll get better."

13. Later Dad died. He was not asleep. He had stopped breathing. He couldn't walk or talk or see any more.

14. The nurse phoned Mum and told her that Dad had died. Mum was very upset.

15. Mum woke Stephen up. She had something very sad to tell him. "Dad won't come home again. He has died."

16. Stephen thought it was a mistake. He wanted to go to the hospital to see Dad. Mum wouldn't let him go. They had an argument.

17. Stephen and Julie didn't feel hungry. They both felt upset.

18. Stephen felt cross and muddled.

19. Stephen thought it must be his fault Dad had gone away. He still didn't believe his Dad was dead.

20. Mum knew why he was upset. She told him again that Dad was dead. Stephen still didn't understand.

21. Next day they went to see Dad. His body was in a coffin. Then Stephen understood that he was dead.

22. Dad's coffin was driven to the cemetery. Stephen, Julie and their Mum came in a different car. Dad's friends came to say goodbye.

23. Everyone said goodbye to Dad. Stephen wondered why Dad had died. Was Dad with God?

24. The curtains closed. Then Dad's body was cremated. It was burnt until only ashes were left.

25. Sometimes Stephen felt lonely. He didn't want to be with his friends. They didn't know what to say. They were glad it wasn't their Dad who had died.

26. Stephen and Julie planted a rose bush with Dad's name on it.

27. Mum gave Stephen and Julie a photograph of Dad to keep. Stephen felt sad all over again. Mum told Stephen that Dad had wanted him to have his watch. That made him feel happy.

28. They were still a family. They had good times together, and they often talked about Dad.

What you can do when someone is very ill

What children can do

Sometimes children aren't allowed to see very ill people, or to go to a funeral (where the dead body is buried in the ground or burnt in a special oven). Then they have to guess or make up a reason for what is going on. The trouble is, when someone is very ill or someone dies everybody else is really upset. If you don't know what happened, because they haven't told you, you will be puzzled about why they are upset. And you won't have a chance to be with the person who is very ill.

People can get worried about what they should say or do when they're with someone ill. Usually it's OK just to be with them, without doing anything special. But if you want to say you love them, or you want to say sorry about something, this may be your last chance to say it.

When someone is dead they're not going to be hurt by being buried or burnt. Sometimes adults think a child is not old enough to understand this. But if you do, you should go to the funeral. This will help you to understand that the person has died. Children can be more frightened if somebody in the family just disappears, and they are never told that the person has died.

What people with learning disabilities can do

If you have a learning disability, that doesn't mean that you should be treated like a child. When someone in your family or your friend is very ill, other people sometimes don't want you to be upset. So they don't tell you what is going on. Or maybe they think that you wouldn't understand, especially if you can't talk properly or you don't know difficult words.

How we feel when someone dies

Most of us don't believe it when we're told that someone has died. We think "It can't be true, it's a mistake." We feel shocked, and sometimes angry. A bit later we feel muddled. Our bodies can also get muddled up after the death of someone we know. We can have headaches, maybe we need to go to the toilet more often, we want to eat a lot or we don't want to eat anything at all and we get a peculiar feeling in the tummy like emptiness or tightness.

Some people want to keep busy and can't sleep, other people can't do anything at all and want to stay in bed all the time. And some people forget how to do things, even things they knew well, like how to get dressed or how to go to the toilet. If we get a pain anywhere we might be scared that we are dying. We have some of these feelings some of the time, and sometimes we feel OK.

Some feelings are upsetting. Anything we see, anything we think about – even a special smell or taste – can remind us of the person who died. Bad memories as well as nice memories pop up, we can feel very scared or very angry. Being angry can happen to anyone. After someone dies we can feel angry with anybody, even with the person who died or other people who love us. And that can make us feel even worse.

We can have dreams about the person who died. Maybe we think we can hear the person who died walking around, or talking to us, or we think we can see them in the street. People worry a lot too. Sometimes they worry that somebody else will die or that it's their fault that the person died.

These strong feelings are called "grief". Grief is not going mad. It is not being bad or naughty. It is OK to feel grief. You know the way your skin fixes itself after you have had a cut? First it bleeds and hurts a lot. Later a lump called a scab covers over the cut. Afterwards there is a mark if the cut was deep. Grief is a bit like that. It is the way that our mind fixes itself after we have been hurt. First it feels very messy and hurts a lot. Then it's more at the back of our minds. Afterwards there is a sad place inside which remembers how much it hurt.

What happens after someone dies

If the person who died was living with you, your life will change in lots of ways. You might even have to move home. You will need time to think and talk about what would be best for you. There shouldn't be any big changes until you have decided.

What about the stuff that belonged to the person who died? Don't throw it all away! Keep things which give you good memories, even if they make you feel sad as well. At the end of the story, Mum, Stephen and Julie go through Dad's things. It makes them feel closer to each other. In the last picture Stephen is holding Dad's watch. When he looks at it he remembers Dad. He feels happy and sad.

What happens to the person who died? We know what happens to their body. It gets buried or burnt. Do you go to a church, a mosque or a synagogue, for example? People who go to these places believe that there is part of every person which is not the body. This part does not die when the body dies. This part is called the soul or spirit or other words which mean the same thing. To find out more about this, ask your family or someone in the place where you go to pray.

How long does it take to get back to normal?

Usually the strong feelings of being sad, angry and muddled get better and worse for a few weeks before they go away. Then there is just a feeling of being sad.

But it can take many months to realise that the dead person will not come back. So sometimes these different feelings, or behaving differently, start many months after the death. This makes it difficult for you and other people to know why you are upset.

For some people life gets back to normal very quickly after somebody else dies. This is OK. Perhaps they knew that the person was going to die, and had lots of sad feelings before the death instead of after it.

For other people the strong feelings come and go for ages – months or even years. Friends and family can get fed up with this. They don't know what to say to you, they feel shy, they don't know what's going on in your mind. But you probably need to talk about the person who died, again and again. Your friends and family need lots of patience! This is what happened to Stephen in the story.

We never completely forget somebody who was close to us. As time goes by we can remember nice things about the person, without being very sad as well. But we still feel a bit sad on birthdays and at the time of year when the person died. We remember them when somebody else dies or when someone gets married or has a baby.

Look at the last picture in the story. The family is smaller but Mum, Julie and Stephen are still together. They are able to talk about Dad. The sun is shining. Everything is OK, even though it is different without Dad.

Where to find help and advice

Cruse Bereavement Care

Central Office   Young people's helpline: 0808 808 1677
Cruse House
126 Sheen Road
Richmond TW9 1UR

Cruse is the national organisation for bereaved people. Some Cruse branches have bereavement supporters who work with children and some who work with people with learning disabilities. Cruse provides information about local bereavement counselling services and also gives welfare advice. The telephone helpline is open Monday to Friday 5.00 pm to 9.00 pm, Saturday 3.00 pm to 5.00 pm and Sunday 3.00 pm to 7.00 pm.

The RD4U is Cruse's young people's website and it can be found at www.rd4u.org.uk. It is designed for young people by young people, and provides support to people after the death of someone close. It has a (monitored) message board and other youthful therapeutic activities, and an email support service run by trained young volunteers. The upper age limit for users of the site is 25 years old.

The Childhood Bereavement Network

8 Wakley Street   Telephone: 020 7843 6309
London EC1V 7QE   email: cbn@ncb.org.uk
    www.ncb.org.uk/cbn

This is a national, multi-agency network of organisations and individuals who work with bereaved children and young people. It includes a growing number of community-based 'open access' services which work with children and young people whatever the cause of their bereavement. These can be searched for on the internet at www.ncb.org.uk/cbn/directory.

It is usually possible to access bereavement counselling through a general practitioner, although this is often very short-term counselling. Many community teams for people with learning disabilities (CTPLDs) can offer bereavement counselling.

It is worth contacting local bereavement counselling services (these should be listed in local telephone directories) to find out whether they offer counselling to people with learning disabilities.

If they do not, this may be because they have never thought about it before. They may be prepared to, but may feel that they do not have enough knowledge. They might want to know more about what it means to have a learning disability and how they might need to extend their skills. They may decide that they would like to have some special training. This could be provided in a number of different ways:

- some advocacy and self-advocacy groups offer training about learning disability
- some community teams for people with learning disabilities provide training
- the training could be provided by a specialist training service.

From 2005, everyone in England who has a learning disability will be encouraged to have a health action plan. A bereavement need could be included in a person's health action plan, which would then mean that they should be supported to get any help that they may need in order to access bereavement counselling.

For more information about health action plans see *Action for Health – Health Action Plans and Health Facilitation*, which contains detailed good practice guidance. Available free from the Department of Health, PO Box 777, London SE1 6XH. An easy-to-read version for people with learning disabilities is also available.

Written information

When Somebody Dies by Sheila Hollins, Sandra Dowling & Noelle Blackman, illustrated by Catherine Brighton. Shows how a man and a woman are helped by regular bereavement counselling sessions, and the comfort and companionship shown by friends, to learn to feel less sad and to cope with life better and better as time passes.

When Mum Died by Sheila Hollins and Lester Sireling, illustrated by Beth Webb. Third edition with new text. The partner book to *When Dad Died*. The book shows a burial. The approach is non-denominational.

Both of the above books are in the Books Beyond Words series (see end of this book).

Am I Allowed to Cry? A Study of Bereavement amongst People who have Learning Difficulties by Maureen Oswin. £12.99. Souvenir Press, London.

Exploring Your Emotions by A. Holland, A. Payne & L. Vickery. A user's manual and set of 30 full-colour photographs illustrating common emotions that can be used in educational and therapeutic settings to help people with learning disabilities learn about their own feelings and the relationship between emotion and behaviour. £25.00 (+£2.50 p&p). British Institute of Learning Disabilities, Wolverhampton Road, Kidderminster, Worcestershire DY10 3PP. Tel: 01752 202 301; fax: 01752 202 333.

Living with Loss: Helping People with Learning Disabilities Cope with Bereavement and Loss edited by Noelle Blackman. £12.95 (+£3.50 p&p). Pavilion Publishing, 8 St George's Place, Brighton, East Sussex BN1 4GB. Tel: 0870 161 3505; fax: 0870 161 3506.

Understanding Death and Dying is a series of three booklets by F. Cathcart to help people with learning disabilities to come to terms with bereavement: *Your

Feelings (illustrated), £3.50 (+£2.40 p&p); *A Guide for Families and Friends*, £4.00 (+£2.50 p&p); and *A Guide for Carers and Other Professionals*, £4.00 (+£2.50 p&p). British Institute of Learning Disabilities (see above for contact details).

Talking Together about Death by J. Cooley & F. McGauran. A bereavement pack containing five sets of sensitively illustrated cards and a user's guide. Designed for both families and carers to share the experience of death and bereavement with people with learning disabilities. £52.82 (incl. VAT). Winslow Press, Telford Road, Bicester, Oxfordshire OX6 0TS.

Loss and Learning Disabilities by Noelle Blackman. This book is for care staff, therapists and counsellors working with people with learning disabilities, showing how they can be affected by bereavement. It includes ways to prevent normal grief from becoming a bigger problem and to help people when the grief process 'goes wrong'. £16.99. Worth Publishing, London.

What on Earth Do You Do When Someone Dies? by Trevor Romain and Elizabeth Verdick. This book aims to help with some of the questions that children struggle with following a bereavement. Each section addresses a different question, including: Why do people have to die? Am I going to die too? Is the death my fault? What can I do if I'm angry? Is it still OK to have fun? The book could be read by an adult to a child, but older children might benefit from reading it on their own. £5.99. Freespirit Publishing, Minneapolis.

Caring for Bereaved Children by Mary Bending. Children feel grief but often show it differently from adults. This concise booklet is for parents, relatives, teachers and others, offering insight into a child's grief and suggesting ways of helping. £2.00 from Cruse Bereavement Care, Cruse House, 126 Sheen Road, Richmond TW9 1UR.

When Someone Dies: Help for Young People Coping with Grief by Dwain Steffes. A practical, sympathetic guide to the often confusing feelings and difficulties young people may experience when grieving. £2.00 from Cruse Bereavement Care, at address on previous page.

Badger's Parting Gifts by Susan Varley. An illustrated book about a wise old badger. When he dies the other animals miss him, but he lives on in all they learned from him. For children under 7 years old. £9.99 from Cruse Bereavement Care, at address on previous page.

When People Die by Sarah Levete. Under headings such as 'What happens when someone dies' and 'Learning to cope' five friends who have each known someone who has died discuss their different feelings and fears. For 8- to 13-year-olds. £5.99. Franklin Watts, London.

Has Someone Died? – Helping Children. A leaflet for parents and carers. Free from Cruse Bereavement Care, at address on previous page.

After Someone Dies A leaflet about death, bereavement and grief for young people of secondary school age. Free from Cruse Bereavement Care, at address on previous page.

Video

Coping with Death. Explains what happens when somebody dies and shows adults with learning disabilities coping with death. £28.00 (incl. p&p) from Speak Up Self Advocacy, 43 Holm Flatt Street, Parkgate, Rotherham, South Yorkshire S62 6HJ. Tel: 01709 7100199; fax: 01709 510009.

Training pack

Understanding Grief: Working with Grief and People Who Have Learning Disabilities by Sheila Hollins & Lester

Sireling. Can be used in formal staff training or as an education tool for families and carers of a bereaved person with a learning disability. This pack includes a video entitled *When People Die* and a copy of the book *When Dad Died*. £70.00 (incl. p&p). Department of Mental Health – Learning Disability, St George's Hospital Medical School, Jenner Wing, Cranmer Terrace, London SW17 0RE. Tel: 020 8725 5496; fax: 020 8672 1070.

Advice for staff supporting adults with learning disabilities

Support staff working in day centres, residential homes or for community support services will find it helpful to have guidelines or procedures to follow when someone dies.

When someone dies who is important to your client (for example, a relative of the client or their keyworker) staff can feel at a loss, and make hasty decisions which they later regret. Various members of staff may offer contradictory advice and guidance to the client. This is why guidelines are helpful, but the guidelines themselves need to be tailored to individual clients.

It is preferable to talk to the client and relatives about their beliefs and wishes regarding death at the initial assessment or soon after acceptance into the service. Guideline questions and a brief questionnaire are provided on the next two pages which can be adapted for your particular organisation. If this discussion is postponed, staff can find themselves having to ask difficult questions at a time of great stress after an unexpected serious illness or death, or staff may have to guess at the wishes of clients and relatives because there is nobody available to provide the information.

Staff sometimes worry that this appears morbid. If asked, carers usually say that they are relieved at the opportunity to discuss their wishes and makes plans. They sometimes admit having worried about what would happen after a bereavement, but have not felt comfortable about discussing this with professionals.

The following questions can be helpful when formulating guidelines

What words, signs or other communication does the client know which will help him or her to understand the concepts of illness or death?

What are the client's cultural and religious beliefs?

What preparation has been carried out by the family or others with regard to education about death?

If the family member or friend is very elderly or ill, is the client aware that the person's death is approaching?

Has the client been bereaved before or been to a funeral or cremation?

Do staff members accompany clients to funerals?

How and when should other clients and staff be informed of the client's bereavement

Should some sort of service or ritual take place in the residential home to mark the death?

What mementos will the client have of the deceased person?

It could be helpful to adapt the questionnaire on the next page for use in your own organisation.

Bereavement questionnaire

Client's name

Address

Name of deceased

Relationship of deceased to client

Date of death

Cause of death

Cremation or burial?

Name and address of cemetery or crematorium

Was funeral or cremation attended? If not give reasons, if known

Has the client been to any other burial or cremation before? Give details

Give details and dates of other important losses

Who does he or she live with?

If different, who did he or she live with before the bereavement?

Give details of important cultural or religious beliefs and traditions

Name of client's own church, temple or synagogue, if any. Give name of contact, if available

Name of general practitioner, social worker or other involved professional

This sheet is excluded from copyright restrictions and may be photocopied

Some other titles in the Books Beyond Words series

Feeling Blue is about a young man who is depressed and has lost interest in things he used to enjoy. This book shows how he is helped to feel better.

Getting On With Cancer is designed to help people who become unwell and are diagnosed as having cancer. Using health services is explained in *Going to the Doctor*, *Going to Out-Patients* and *Going into Hospital*.

Looking After My Breasts and *Keeping Healthy 'Down Below'* are about breast and cervical screening.

Getting on with Epilepsy shows that people with epilepsy can enjoy an active and independent life.

Looking After My Balls shows young men with learning disabilities how to check their testicles to look for anything that may be wrong, and to seek help from their GP if they are worried.

Mugged tells what happens to a young man after he is attacked in the street. It includes suggestions for role-playing different responses to unwelcome approaches from strangers.

The difficult subject of sexual abuse is covered in *Jenny Speaks Out*, *Bob Tells All* and *I Can Get Through It*. The third title shows how a woman who has been abused is helped to get through the experience with the help of regular counselling and psychotherapy.

Speaking Up for Myself shows how people with learning disabilities from ethnic minority groups have the right to challenge discrimination.

Three books cover access to criminal justice as a victim (witness) or as a defendant: *Going to Court*, *You're Under Arrest* and *You're on Trial*.

Food . . . Fun, Healthy and Safe shows how choosing, cooking and eating food can be fun as well as healthy and safe. Included are do's and don'ts to prevent choking, general advice on eating well and outlines of special diets.

Michelle Finds a Voice shows how Michelle and her carers are helped to overcome her difficulties in communication. Various solutions are explored, including the use of signing, symbols and charts.

Peter's New Home and *A New Home in the Community* help people to make a happy transition to a new home.

Forming new relationships is the subject of three books: *Making Friends* tells the story from a man's point of view, and *Hug Me, Touch Me* tells the story from a woman's perspective. *Falling in Love* traces the ups and downs of a romantic relationship.

Two books about personal care are *George Gets Smart* and *Susan's Growing Up.* The latter tells the story of a young girl's first menstruation.

To order copies (at £10.00 each; 10% reduction for 10 or more books) or for a leaflet giving more information, please contact: Book Sales, Royal College of Psychiatrists, 17 Belgrave Square, London SW1X 8PG. Credit card orders can be taken by telephone (020 7235 2351, extension 146).